Gary McNair

MCGONAGALL'S CHRONICLES (WHICH WILL BE REMEMBERED FOR A VERY LONG TIME)

OBERON BOOKS
LONDON

WWW.OBERONBOOKS.COM

Writer's Note

Dear Reader,

There's something I'd like to make clear before I go on in case you are not aware of it – William McGonagall was a real person. It may seem at times like he is a character plucked from my wildest imagination. He is not. For me this show only works because he is real. If I were to create a bad poet from your mind, they could never be as perfect as him. He is the stuff of reality, which makes him all the more unbelievable to us.

As you'll see in the prologue, I was introduced to William McGonagall a few years ago by a friend. I'd bumped into him in the street and we had an impromptu coffee to catch up. I told him I was writing a play about a bad comedian (*Donald Robertson is Not A Standup Comedian,* also available from the wonderful people at Oberon) and he said 'I take it you're a fan of McGonagall?' I said "Who's McGonagall?" His face lit up with that joy that people's faces light up with when they realise they get to introduce someone to something brilliant that they know that person will love. Then he read me 'The Tay Bridge Disaster' and the rest is history. Needless to say it started a bit of an obsession for me with the poet. I immediately shared that obsession with my brother Ross, who I thought would love McGonagall's poetry both because of his brilliant sense of humour and the fact that he has lived in Dundee since the turn of the Millennium. We took great pleasure in unearthing more and more of McGonagall's poetic gems and reading about the truly bizarre elements of his biography.

At first we were just amused and amazed by it all but soon I realised that I really loved this guy. There was something about him and his story that you won't find in any other historical character.

I think he captures something about the true spirit of an artist. He never mingled in high society, he had no contacts or connections to publishing, he was a working man who turned to his passion in an attempt to survive when the industry of his city collapsed. It would have been hard for anyone to say outright that he was good at poetry – he does deserve his title of 'world's worst poet' but while others starved waiting around for weaving work that was not to come, he found a way to survive.

I love that there is something quintessentially Scottish about him and his story, yet he is unlike any other Scottish figure I've ever read about. I realised it was time to try and tell his story.

I first tried to achieve this as one short poem – 'An Ode To McgOnagall'. The great late theatre producer David MacLennan booked it in as a three minute curtain raiser at A Play, Pie and A Pint at Òran Mór in Glasgow. In true McGonagall style it lasted seven minutes. Afterward, delighted with how it was received, David told me that it was "bloody marvellous". I replied by saying "thanks, so … do you want to book the full length version?" David, without a moments hesitation, replied with his famous perfect timing "not a fucking chance!" If it had come from anyone else you might have felt a little hurt by such a put down. But from David, it wasn't a put down, it was a challenge, a motivating gesture. It was also a stark warning that, if I were to stretch the piece from seven minutes to an hour and try to retain they joy that it would need a lot of work. Sadly David passed away a few years ago but I'm pleased that we were able to give the show it's premier at Òran Mór where it all began with him and I like to think he would have loved the show.

I hope you love it too. And I hope it leads you to loving the work of William McGonagall. I love his poetry, as undeniably bad as it is. I love it. There's an honesty to it that you don't find in many places.

We've included a few of his poems here in this book to kick start your passion but I strongly recommend you get his complete works, it's a joy. There is also a brilliant biography by Norman Watson which proved invaluable when writing this play. It's well worth a read.

I've also included a few poems which I like to call Modern McGonagalls – a series of poems I have been writing as a side project to this play where I try to summon the spirit of McGonagall and imagine what he would make of events in the world today. I encourage you to do the same.

Thanks for reading

Gary

Director's Note

Working with Gary McNair is like trying to catch a wasp with your teeth without biting it in two. Don't push it too hard or question why you're doing what you're doing, or you'll end up with a tongue that's too fat for your mouth. Usually from the inordinate amount of sugar that's consumed in his rehearsal rooms.

Gary thinks quickly in an almost back to front way. He's illogical yet speaks sense. He has a well-honed understanding of story and a knack for expression that almost always surprises. He doesn't seem to care what people think, firmly focused on his words (often puns) both written and performed. Sound like anyone we know?

The subject of William Topaz McGonagall – as chronicled by Gary McNair – is one of those ideas that seems too perfect. Two perennial jesters, both with a love of language and an audience's attention, both with an innate understanding of what the audiences want but unafraid to take them on, both with a devil inside them that makes them go "fuck it, let's walk" when Balmoral is a hundred miles away through the pissing rain...

The reconfiguring of McGonagall as a working class folk hero – as opposed to purely a figure of fun – will take more than one play. But this story will add to the cannon. And his doggerel surely deserves another look, if for no other reason than the unbridled joy his work brings; eliciting strong reactions is rare, the preserve of artists who have captured an essence of themselves and what it is to be human in their work. And McGonagall gives us the truth, flaws and all.

Creating this show with Gary (with Simon Liddell and Brian O'Sullivan and the tireless team at A Play, a Pie & a Pint) was bittersweet, as I knew it would be my last one in Scotland for a while. I was living in Dundee and often thought of McGonagall, staring out over the "silvery" expanse and the immortalised rail bridge. What would he make of Dundee and all the changes? As Gary's play articulates, here was a weaver who couldn't work as the industry changed around him, so he resolutely grafted on his words and his performances. Nowhere better exemplifies that spirit of graft within Scottish Theatre than A Play, a Pie & a Pint at Òran Mór, brainchild of the late, great David Maclennan, who gave both Gary and me early breaks in our career. We have both learned from the best in how to duck and dive and thrive on our ideas and ability to convince other people to join us in doing silly things. Perhaps if McGonagall had more regular, supportive patronage, like the kind we got from Dave, he would've had more permission to be silly. And been able to develop more fully as an artist too.

Creative Team

Gary McNair, Writer and Performer

Gary McNair is a writer and performer
Whose hair is naturally curled
He's been lucky enough to win a few awards
And perform around the world

He studied theatre at the RCS
When it was called the academy
Where he learned to contemplate the void
And ponder the state of humanity

Since then he's written many plays
A few of which were rubbish
But Oberon think that seven of them
Were good enough to publish

His plays have taken many forms
Though this is his first in verse
He's writer in residence at the National Theatre of Scotland
And an Associate Artist at The Traverse

If you'd like to know any more such as where you can watch
one of his plays
Then why not take a moment out of your day
To follow him on Twitter* or visit his website at
www.garymcnair.co.uk

*@thegarymcnair

Joe Douglas, Director

Watch our show and you must wholeheartedly agree
Any old tumshee
Could've directed this stramash
So go on yersel. Give it a bash.

It's more than just tellin em where to stand
You have to think of things to say that are profound.
Joe has directed loads in Scotland, up in Bonnie Dundee on the Silvery Tay
Some Roald Dahls, Brecht and that Death of a Salesman play
But most famously was probably his toil
Directing the Cheviot, the Stag and the Black, Black Oil.

He was often blessed
To work everywhere from a Play, a Pie & a Pint to the NTS.
But now he's away to Live Theatre in The Toon,
Newcastle's not far though, come away doon.

Simon Liddell, Composer/Musician

Simon Liddell is a musician
And a sound designer
The likes of which you will not find
Anywhere that is finer

He toured with Frightened Rabbit for years
Across the world they would make fans cheer
He plays an innumerable amount of instruments
He can rock out and makes sounds that are intimate

Notes, chords, he knows them all
But it doesn't mean he'll use them
He'll pick out just the right ones
And with the words he'll fuse them

So if you want a full soundtrack
Or if you need musical support just a little
You could do a whole lot fucking worse
Than employing Simon Liddell

Brian James O'Sullivan, Musician and Chorus.

From knee-high to a grasshopper and a very young age
Brian wanted nothing more than to be on the stage
He made up wee shows, dragged his parents along
Enchanted them weekly with sketch and with song

As the years they did pass, his passion continued
But never for dance 'cos he wasn't that sinewed
He hit Òran Mór at the top of the Byres
Having not done all that well in his highers

Since then he has acted, he's sung and he's played
And is able to answer yes when members of his extended family ask
"do you get paid?"
He's travelled, he's met folk, he's eaten nice food
But he feels most at home in his wee flat in Knightswood

He's been called rising star, numpty and chancer
And often plays music for young Irish dancers
But nothing compares to the thrill, oh so rare
Of sharing the stage with his pal Gary McNair

Tomaž Krajnc, Assistant Director

Tomaž Krajnc is a young director
whose stock is on the rise
In his short career he's won some awards
which is hardly a surprise

Born and raised in Celje,
Which is a lovely city in Slovenia
Where, before he came to Scotland to study Theatre
He got a degree in psychology where he studied conditions like schizophrenia

He thinks that degree is useful
When he's directing plays
As he can make break throughs with the actors
After he's analysed their ways.

When studying here
It was clear
That his talents were rather special
We all agree that he'll go on to direct at the highest level

He may one day direct the theatrical
Equivalent of the Mona Lisa
But thanks to the backward thinking shit bin that is Brexit
We'll never see his work again without a visa!

McGonagall's Chronicles (Which Will Be Remembered For A Very Long Time) was first performed on 26 March, 2018 as part of A Play, A Pie and A Pint at Òran Mór.

Directed by Joe Douglas
Sound design and composition by Simon Liddell

Cast: Gary McNair, Brian James O'Sullivan and Simon Liddell

This publication is released as the production returns to the Traverse on 5 December 2018 for a run of ten performances before starting its onward touring which will begin at the Tron Theatre, Glasgow in January of 2019 as part of Celtic Connections.

Dedicated to the memory of William McGonagall. Thanks for the joy. Thanks for the words.

Thanks to

Dave Arthur
Katy McNair
Ross McNair
Dave MacLenan
Everyone at Play, Pie and A Pint
Everyone at The Traverse
Emily Hickman
Georgie Smith
The Agency
Joe Douglas
Brian O'Sullivan
Simon Liddell
Carrie Taylor
George Spender and all at Oberon

Pre Show Announcement

CHORUS: Ladies and gentlemen Some housekeeping:
    No burping no farting and please – no sleeping
    And if you *must* sleep – please no snoring
    No shouting or talking, even if this is boring
    I hope you'll have a laugh or two
    But I'll be honest you shouldn't expect it
    You might want to take this chance to head for the exit
    And you'll need those if there's a fire so look for the doors with
    the green lights which are up at the back and here to my right
    And if you do hate it and you want to leave
    You can do something better like go to bed early
    Or you could go have a nice dinner and come back and see the
    other play that's on tonight – *Mouthpiece* by Kieran Hurley*[1]

    Phones off, right off, so they have no power
    Don't worry I promise, you'll be out in an hour
    And at times, yes, it may feel impossibly longer
    Well tough! What doesn't kill you will only make you stronger.

    Ach what am I talking about
    I want you to scream and shout
    If you think the show's rubbish
    Tell us, let it out
    Better still if you've brought things to throw
    Chuck at the actors, go on, give it a go!
    Not now, good people, have some decorum
    When this plumb comes out to perform his daft poem
    And seriously, if you do think it's boring
    We can chase him off stage and kick his dressing room door in!

---

1   This rhyme was in reference to the next play to be performed in the
    presenting theatre at the time of printing, it will change as the play
    travels. Have fun creating you own.

Prologue

NARRATOR: Gather round friends, I'll tell you a story
I promise you it's not all jackanory
I was walking one day down a Glasgow street
When I saw a friend I was most delighted to meet
We went for a quick coffee
And caught up with each other
We ended up having such an awfy
Good time we stayed for another

He told me he'd been enjoying a poet recently

CHORUS: "Would you like to have a listen?"

NARRATOR: Eh… no really

CHORUS: "Ah go on. You don't know what you're missing!"

NARRATOR: Then, right before my eyes
Much to my upmost surprise
He read me a poem
And it made me cry

Not because it was moving
Or particularly sad
I was crying from laughter
Because it was so terribly bad

And it was no short poem
I'd say it was sizeable
The meter was off, none of it scanned

The syntax was completely unrecognisable

In fact, the only part of it that seems to make it qualify as
a poem, and this bit's truly sublime
Was the writer's sheer gallus ability to shorten or lengthen
the last line of a stanza so that it could end with a thumping
rhyme

"No one could be this bad", I did think
A gaff like this must be a one-off, a fluke
But then my friend took me back to his flat for a drink
Where he presented me with a book

We spend the night laughing,
oh how we had a blast
As we struggled to understand the motivations for this man's
tomb of work, where each poem was as bad as the last

Who was this guy? Was it meant to be funny?
Was he meant to be bad? Did he make any money?
And the more you try to answer all this
The more quandaries you're presented with
Like; was he for real, was he desperate, was it a hoax, did
he have additional learning support needs, was he bad on
purpose to turn a buck, was he a genius, was he an idiot...
what did it all mean?
And what kind of a mental strain did this put on his long
suffering wife, Jean?

Some of these questions we'll answer
Though some will prove impossible
Come with us now as we attempt to chronicle
The life and times of sir William Topaz McGonagall

A SONG: 'McGonagall, McGonagall'

(Verse 1)

McGonagall, McGonagall
He truly was phenomenal

McGonagall, McGonagall
He faced many obstacles

But McGonagall, McGonagall
Was a force that was unstoppable

McGonagall, McGonagall
To him, his poetical call was not optional

(Chorus 1)
Oh come away to the braes
Of the Silvery Tay

(Verse2)
McGonagall, McGonagall
At times found life impossible

McGonagall, McGonagall
Left marks that are unwahshable

McGonagall, McGonagall
With his life I'll be methodical

McGonagall, McGonagall
To not tell his story would be irresponsible

4

(Chorus 2)
Oh come away to the braes
Of the Silvery Tay

(Verse 3)
McGonagall, McGonagall
Some of his poetry was abominable

But McGonagall, McGonagall
Achieved great fame in Scotland, where he was domicile

McGonagall, McGonagall
Is sill known round the world
From Dundee to Dheli
From Darfur to Dakota
From Detroit to Denmark
From Damascus to Denver
Form Dortmund to Dubai
From Dijon to Dublin
From Dallas to Dingwall
From Danyang to Donegal

We hereby bring his chronicles
Of sir William Topaz McGonagall

SONG ENDS

*

Parents and early life

NARRATOR: This is the story of an unschooled, unskilled, low paid
hand loom weaver
That goes on to be a global praise receiver
The Victorian, non Etonian, honorary Dundonian down his
tools at fifty-two, then travel further than Napoleon
This poor weaver Caledonian, quits the loom for a life of a
stentorian

CHORUS: What are you saying, that he somehow became a Roman
soldier?
Is that not a stentorian? Oh, is it a foul mythical beast? Oh
no, is it something bleaker?

NARRATOR: No. It's a public speaker!

And leaves behind a story that has baffled most historians

Come sit by the fire,
But please do not touch the hearth
And I will tell you the story
Of McGonagall's birth

He was not born in a lab in a flask that was conical
But from the womb of the rather lovely Mrs McGonagall

To tell you the year it happened, or the place it took place
I'm not really able
For the year it happened and the place it took place
Are somewhat debatable

For these facts, along with how his name is spelled or
even pronounced
Are all things for which McGonagall gave
Throughout his life, many different accounts

We'll get to the where and when in a moment
But if first you'll have some patience
I'll give a brief biography of his parents

His dad was born in Ireland
Where he spent most of his life
So was his mother
Who was his father's wife

From their responsibilities they would never shirk
They both bade farewell to the green isle
In search of weaving work

The search for employment
Was indeed so thorough
That it took them from Ireland
All the way to Edinburgh

This is where most accounts say William came to be alive
And the year is generally accepted as 1825

In Edinburgh, his folks worked hard, kept their heads
down
And never got an ASBO
But their luck ran out and the work dried up
And they had to move to Glasgow

They hit the road again.
Got as far as Orkney, near Shetland
But this was another place
In which they did not feel like settling

They had this pattern
Settle, flee, settle, flee, settle, flee, settle, flee
Until they reached the beautiful city of bonnie Dundee

Dundee

If you were a weaver in Dundee around 1847
You'd think you'd have died and gone to heaven
For in the mid 1800's
This fine city had a weaving boom bringing jobs in abundance

But that didn't mean that life wasn't easy
All that factory smoke could sure make you queasy

William, as a child, was bonnie and gay
He took every chance he could to sport and play
As children do, that is their way

He did enjoy school and by his own claim did show
great potential
But we'll sadly never know what academic heights he would
have reached for the family needed him to go to work and so,
at age seven, was pulled out of school which was seen as 'non-
essential'

So to keep up rent on their dank, crumbling room.
William McGonagall not even eight years old was sent to
the loom

He was nimble and quick.
He fair took to the job
And to the family purse
He would have added a few bob

As time went on, he kept on growing until he was fully grown
He got on with life, he met his wife and had children of his own.
And just like him, they had to work, but they didn't
complain, they all understood
It was essential, well, if they wanted food.

And that's that.
For forty years things largely stayed the same.
If he'd died when he was fifty
The world would never have known his name

Forty years of grind
And forty years of toil
Worked into the ground
Buried in the soil

Two score year and ten
Just like my father got
Just like his father before him
All happy with their lot

Forty years of toil
And forty years of grind
We'll work our days
For meagre pay
And our names get left behind

For the only dreams around
Are the men's whose wealth we build
The men up at the top
Who got their pockets filled

All men live
And all men pass
You seldom get a story
If you're from the working class

Yes all men live
And all men pass
But you seldom get a story
If you're from the working class

SONG ENDS

William the Actor

So if he died here in early 1877
We probably wouldn't know his name
But that doesn't mean he hadn't ever had
A shot at fame.

CHORUS: What?

NARRATOR: His hobby

CHORUS: What? Tennis? Skiing? Acrobatics?

NARRATOR: No, I mean his time in amateur dramatics.

Back in 1858 he first tried to show the world his greatness

CHORUS: With about as much success as a football team from
Caithness

NARRATOR: It was the height of the weaving boom
And with it there was culture
Theatres and music halls sprung up everywhere
To entertain the workers

Him and his pals would go to the theatre of a night
And he thought:
"Some of these actors are... sub par"

If someone would give him a go on stage
His career was sure to take off

He was bound to be as popular as *Game of Thrones*
Or the great *British Bake Off*
He'd be as big as the post war radio stations
Or Kevin Spacey…
Before the allegations

Picture the scene – the house is filled
It's absolutely packed to the gills
McGonagall is to play Macbeth
Who, spoiler alert, Macduff is supposed to kill

But he's having such a good time on the stage
That he felt it would be a shame to send his character to the grave.
He strutted and weaved about with great swagger
Dodging every swipe of Mcduff's sword and dagger.

But in disbelief his co-workers cheered on this bizarrity

CHORUS: *'Get intae him, McGonagall'*

NARRATOR: And they fell about with the utmost hilarity

His fellow actor to say the least was ragin'

CHORUS: Go down you damn fool!
This is not the agreed staging

NARRATOR: And while he'd made the audience bend over so much
with laughter
They might require a chiropractor
This did spell the end of his time as an actor

And this would not be the last time he misunderstood

Thee jeers of bullies as proof that he was good.
But McGonagall did not dismay
"The world would know my name one day"

*

Epiphany

So at the age of fifty-two
Twenty years on from from that stage debut

The reality was getting harder to disguise
The truth that was before Dundee's eyes
The weaving boom was now in great demise
For mechanisation was on the rise

With work drying up, his age was proving to be a menace
Fifty-two was to old to become an apprentice
And he had not the skills to become a farmer or a dentist

The City was slumping the mood was down
People were hungry all over town
Books were getting harder to balance
But this is where the great McGonagall would come in to his
own, he would aim to survive on his god-given talents

For he'd tasted fame and its intoxicating flavour
"This is a flavour I would once again love to savour"

CHORUS: Mate – I think a Dundonian pronounce that word
"seevour"?

NARRATOR: Either way, he was done with being a weaver!

If he could not get himself back on the stage
He would make a name for himself on... the page!

He'd proved himself a writer before
Oh with pride it did make his heart to soar
When his theatrical critique of a famous actor was printed in
the paper
"Perhaps I could repeat this caper"

What else could he critique?
Dickens? Shakespeare? The album of the week?
No! He felt that he should have ambitions greater
Than simply being a mere commentator.

A side note: That was purely McGonagall's view
To any reviewers in the house, I respect, cherish and value you.

"Perhaps I could make people grovel
At my feet if I wrote the world's greatest novel"

But that would be an awful lot of work,
Plus think of all that paper
It could easily got lost or mixed up,
As this was long before the invention of the ring binder, or
the stapler!

"A novel would take far to long
I know! I could try writing a song!"

Two main factors took this option from his hand
He couldn't play an instrument and he didn't have a band.

"If only there were songs that didn't need not to be sung"
This is when his creative life truly begun!

Strike up the band, roll the timpani's
It's time for the moment of McGonagall's epiphany

"I am going to have a go at…
Writing words that ryhme so I can show that…
I am gifted! And soon everyone will know it…
I am a… writer of poetry!"

Enraptured, enthralled, he began to write
He took to it full pelt that very night
For inspiration he went for a wander
Wondering whom he would most like to honour

So he thought as he wondered, he wondered and he
walked
He walked and he pondered, he pondered and he thought
He thought of all the good people he did ken
Searching for someone to immortalise with his pen

*"Who is it that I should honour in rhyme
And will therefor be remembered… for a very long time.
Mater? Pater?
No, my thunderous poetical debut must focus on someone greater*

*I could think of no greater a man
Greater even than Peter Pan
Than my Favourite Reverend
Mr George Gilfillan"*

So he wrote straight away with his pencil, filled with lead
He wrote all day and all night until he went to his bed
And when he woke in the morning and his bedclothes were
shed

And he'd eaten his breakfast so that he was fed
He agreed it was time for his work to be read
So he read it to his wife and this is what she probably said…

CHORUS: Oh aye, that's em… alright?
Erm… Did that take you all night?

NARRATOR: Not to be dismayed, and still imbued
by his muse
He dropped it off anonymously at the offices of
the Weekly News,
Where his ode to the famous reverend
Was printed the following weekend

He was excited, delight and filled with glee
And was sure this proved the world's greatest poet was he

But to assure their readers that their high standards for
the weekly poetry column hadn't slipped
They also printed a cheap dig at the anonymous writer, here
is their quip

CHORUS: *'WMG of Dundee, who modestly seeks to hide his light under
a bushel, has surreptitiously dropped into our letter box an address
to Rev George Gilfillan. Here is a sample of the worthy's power of
versification'*

NARRATOR: They were aiming, I think, to cause him humiliation

But if they were hoping to put him off, they seemed to do
it too discretely
Because of course McGonagall, delighted to be in print,
missed their point completely

And from their swiping comment he sees no condemnation
And takes the whole thing as pure validation

"This surely proves I am one of the greats
Like my heroes; Tannahill, Tennyson and Yates"

CHORUS: Here you! This was 1877 and while Yates was
indeed alive
He didn't have anything published till 1885

NARRATOR: Look, I know this was before Yates' time
But I defy anyone to pass up that rhyme

CHORUS: And another thing, Tanahil was the Poet Laureate
McGonagall wisnea
That's like me spray painting a cock on the toilet wall
And stotin about like I'm Disnae

NARRATOR: *"Well I know I have some work to be done*
To prove I am poet numero one.
If I'm to show the world I am Tanahill's equal
I must first get to work on a splendorous sequel"

He followed it up with a poem about the Tay bridge
Which was truly awful
It mainly focused on the fact that it was big
And that he hoped it would not fall
And amazingly, once again, he was committed to print
And his local legend status was starting to cement

So he wrote and he wrote and he wrote and he wrote
And he wrote and he wrote and he wrote and he wrote
And he wrote and he wrote and he wrote and he wrote
And this is the kind of feedback he got

CHORUS: *'Reader you'll struggle to relax*
When you bear witness to McG's syntax
Needing a laugh, here's the solution
Have a wee gander at his latest effusion
Readers please take this latest rhyme As proof that his work does not
improve over time'

NARRATOR: He was now untethered, there was nothing
could slow him
He hugely accelerated the rate at which he wrote poems
And of course he increased the paper and their reader's fun
When his poems started being signed by:
William McGonogall, Poet to the Queen...
here's what he'd done

First Royal Patronage

While people laughed at his work,
His situation wasn't funny
He had a family to feed
And he wasn't making any money

He survived on borrowed money that anyone would
lend him
But he knew he could make a living from his poetry if he
could capitalise on his momentum

From poverty's clutches, the quickest removal
He felt, was to write to the Queen requesting royal approval

So on a wing and a prayer
And a heart full of hope
He put some sample poems
Into an envelope

He sent it off to the Queen at her castle
With a letter requesting royal recognition, if it wasn't too
much hassle.
And though it may have seemed a little pie in the sky
Would you believe it
'I GOT A REPLY!'

Imagine a scene in a tenement flat
You've come in the door,
You've removed your jacket
you've taken off your gloves and also your hat

You've wiped your shoes on the mat

You've bent at the knee
and also at the back
To pick up some mail
That had come from a postman's sack

An ordinary scene
happens most every day
Apart from the days when you are away

So, imagine how you would have felt
As he was down on his knee, or you could say, knelt

I imagine you would feel incredibly braw
It's the kind of moment you wish could have been
witnessed by your parents

And what did the letter say?
Well, it clearly said she had no time for unsolicited poems
but he did not dismay

If you could read the letter. Please, immerse us...

CHORUS: The Private Secretary is commanded by THE QUEEN to
thank Mr W McGonagall for his letter with the enclosed verses
but////

NARRATOR: *'Ah ha!!! "Commanded BY THE QUEEN to THANK ME for
the VERSES"*

Honestly, who cares what the rest says!'

That first bit of the letter, he must have taken to heart
And for what he did next, you have to give him credit
Because he threw away the second part
That said she hadn't read it.

So he took that first sentence.for that first sentence that
thanked him for his poetry was real.

And inscribed it on all his future works, along with the
royal seal

Self Published Pamphlets

Now it was certain that wherever he'd go
He'd boast his royal patronage far and wide
Now there was nothing now that could deflate his ego

CHORUS: And bloody hell, folk tried

NARRATOR: Oh yes, though he was on a relentless poetical mission
    Eventually the papers grew tired of his constant submissions
    And they hoped he'd take the hint
    When they more or less stopped committing any of his poems
    to print

CHORUS: McGonagall, thanks for all the poems you've given us
    You've delighted something we didn't know we had in us
    We gave you a shout out, as we laughed at first
    But things have truly gone from bad to verse
    So no hard feelings, I hope you'll thank us for the journey,
    but it ends here, I hope you'll agree it's been fun.

NARRATOR: *"It ends here? Pah! My journey has only just begun*
    You can't keep me down
    Do you not remember my Macbeth?
    Hell, I could even play Hamlet?
    I shall publish my work myself,
    And charge sixpence for the pamphlet"

You see, he had an ounce of fame
And he was eager to exploit it
So he could make money off his name
But he may already have spoiled it

For this pamphlet of poems rather than bring him his
desired fortune
Took him to debtors' court for a formal caution:

CHORUS: *"Sir, if only you would go to work*
       Instead of writing poetry
       Then you would not be here in court
       For me to have a go at you"

NARRATOR: *"Your honour, if you would give me the room*
       I daresay it must me said
       That there is such meagre work for my hand at the loom
       That I am having to use my head"

CHORUS: *"Sir, of your poems I hear there is quite the reputation*
       And I fear you may have ideas above your station
       I hear they are awful, and though you are jeered on by some
       This court cannot possibly see them providing an income"

NARRATOR: *"And what, sir, do you suggest I do to escape this gloom?*
       Do you know of another industrial boom?
       Should I perhaps create my own loom?
       Should I charter voayages from Dundee to the moon?"

CHORUS: *"Enlist for work*
       I urge you show willing
       Or so help me for your debt
       I'll charge a pound on each shilling"'

NARRATOR: *"Well, bang down your gavel*
       Wield your power like Macduff's sword
       But there's nothing can unravel
       the power of my words

You say there's nothing to be earned by a working class poet?
Well, I say there is and I'm going to show you this"

What is Genius[2]

What is genius?
Tis a thing seldom rewarded;
If you are in poverty
Tis sure to be disregarded
But if you are a rich man
Your company is courted
By the high and low,
Throughout all the world wherever you go.
Whereas the poor man
By his fellow workman is spurned;
They look upon him with a jealous eye
And their noses upturned,
And they say to themselves,
You are no greater than we;
If you are, show it,
And we'll all worship ye.
And rally around you,
And applaud you to the skies;
And none of us all
Will you ever despise
Because you can help yourself,
You are a very great man,
And everyone of us
Will do all that we can,
You for to please,

---

2 'What is Genius' is the only original McGonagall to feature in the play. We added it because it is unlike his other poems in the doggerel style. It's sweet and sensitive and speaks to the pain of a working-class artist. It was never published in his collective works. We came across it in Norman Watson's brilliant biography. In the staging, I read it from a piece of paper that we have placed inside his collected works as our way of saying that it should be remembered as well as the rest of his poems.

And never will tease,
Nor try to offend you
By any misbehaviour;
And to court your favour
We will always endeavour.
That is the way genius
Is rewarded;
But if you are in poverty
Tis sure to be disregarded

Balmoral

It's now the year 1878
And our poet, still trying to prove he is one of the greats
Concocts a plan that is at least sure
To enter him into chancer's folklore

He'd prove to that judge there was money to be gleaned
If he could get himself an audience with the Queen

But here's the perfect dilemma:
To perform for the Queen would give him a reputation and money
But he couldn't afford to go see her as it was something he
currently had none eh.

He couldn't afford a train
He had no personal transport of which to talk
So even though there was torrential rain
There was only one thing for it – *'Fuck it, I'll walk'*

So he sets off on foot with spirits miraculously high
Heading from Dundee to Balmoral which is about the same
distance as from Inverness over to Skye
As the crow flies

For the sixty miles it poured, soaking him through, a real tragedy
For he wanted to be nothing but presentable for her majesty
It's hard to think of an achievement greater
Than when tired but not defeated, he reached the castle about
two days later

He dusts off his kilt, asks politely to see the queen
But her guardsmen did refuse his request to seen

CHORUS: *"So you're this poet? Right then, show us your poetical worth."*

NARRATOR: *"Well, if I'm to perform for anyone, they must fatten my purse."*

[A PHYSICAL MOMENT. THE GUARD MAKES IT CLEAR THAT HIS REQUEST FOR MONEY HAS NOT GONE OVER WELL]

"And out here? In the open air?
I would not even perform in such conditions for Her Majesty
Let alone for you two, you miserable pair"

It was at that moment he firmly ran out of luck
As they firmly told him that he should get tae ...

CHORUS: *"REMOVE YOURSELF"*

NARRATOR: He figured there was surely nothing could be done
So he bade them farewell and he just goes home

*

So what do we learn from his trip to Balmoral?
What is the takeaway, what is the moral?
He gave it a shot and he went back home
That's not giving up, that's moving on

****

Performance Poet

The papers delighted that he was snubbed by the Queen,
though they were impressed by how far he walked
And with his growing reputation he could just about scrape by
With the money from the pamphlets that he hawked.

But there had to be a way to earn a decent wage

"Of course, I must take my poetry to the stage"

One night he secured a venue
With a deposit of a shilling or two

Then he paid to have an announcement made by the town cryer
Which is bit like Victorian Twitter
But after he took his money, he just pissed off which was a bit
of a shitter

He played a few more gigs but he was hardly in demand
But to propel him to stardom fate played a strange hand.

Remember his second poem An Ode to the Tay Bridge
He prayed no disaster would befall the passengers, it was right
there in stanza six

And so he could not have been the only one who gasped
When the great, grand central girders did collapse

The City was grieving,

They knew not where to turn

CHORUS: What about McGonagall
        Could he be the one?

NARRATOR: *"I feel this city's grief with you all.*
        To mark this tragedy, I will proudly answer the call!"

He took his paper and pencil and sat up on Dundee Law
And wrote a poem so bad it would unlock your jaw

Despite it being about the death of ninety people
It's so funny it would make your mind boggle
Honestly, if you've never read it,
Do yourself a favour when you get home and look it up on
Google

After the Tay Bridge Disaster things were never the same
It was printed up and down the country he was now a
household name

Now if he played in the back of a pub
Or a venue the size of the coliseum
If he was on the bill
People turned out in their droves to see him

But all this stardom came at a price
For the audiences who came were never nice
They were really much more of a mob than a crowd
They were hurling abuse that was deafeningly loud

He mustn't have been surprised that the lampooning he
received in the paper's pages

Would set the tone for how he would be treated on the
city's stages

And if the papers would report the night's mistreatment
The audience saw it as a great achievement

CHORUS: *"Come on lads, it will be a great night out*
He'll make an arse of himself and we can scream and shout
I guarantee it will NOT be boring
And if it is, we can just chase him off the stage and kick his dressing
room door in"

NARRATOR: So here he is presented with a Catch 22
And I put it to you

Is there anyone out there thinks they could handle
These ruffians, roustabouts and boisterous vandals
Would you go out everynight and take abuse on stage
If it was your only way of getting a wage?

Gullable Mcgonagall

And it was not just on stage he was the victim of jokes
He was a soft touch, a gullible man, an easy target for a hoax

He received a rail ticket in the post
With a letter that insisted
That he travel straight away to some far off town
To open a theatre that never existed

He'd be told he was to perform alongside a famous
travelling actor, though his name would not be listed
And when he turned up early and eager for his slot
They'd tell him he'd already missed it

People said he must be as mad as a cuckoo
When he believed he was being wined and dined by
Ireland's great playwright Dion Boucicault

CHORUS: *"I'd like to offer you a role in my touring production
For an astronomical fee"*

NARRATOR: And he was truly sucked in

You'd think he'd cotton on but nope
He was a man who lived in hope

He was deeply saddened by this hoax most fowl
It did make him cry and make him howl
It made his head spin and wonder deliriously

How no one would take him, as he'd taken these pranksters,
seriously
But something nice happened that lightened his woe
Having heard of the hoax, the real Boucicault,
Sent him a nice letter with a fiver in toe

This was a rather substantial amount
About six weeks weaving wages at his last count

In light of this most generous funding
He figured that people must be nicer in London
So, though it was incredibly bold
He left for the capital where he hoped the streets would be
paved with gold

Travel Tales

"CRUEL CITIZENS OF DUNDEE
I NOW MUST BID FAREWELL TO YE
I AM GOING TO LONDON FAR AWAY
WHEN I WILL RETURN I CANNOT SAY
FAREWELL TO THE BANKS OF THE SILVERY TAY
AND THE BEAUTIFUL HILL O' BALGAY
AND ILL FATED BRIDGE OF SILVERY TAY
I WILL REMEMBER YOU WHEN FAR AWAY
AND IF I EVER SEE DUNDEE AGAIN
I HOPE IT IS WITH THE LAURELS OF FAME"

CHORUS: To put it politely his time in London could have been greater
For he was shunned and he returned only three days later
And if you think that move was a little unorthodox
He did the same thing three years later with bloody NEW
YORK!

NARRATOR: Yes he woke up one morning and said *"er a car"*
That would take him to the train that would take him to the
boat that would take him to America

Yes, he headed to the place where Autumn is called Fall
With big dreams of performing at Carnegie Hall

It seems impossible for me to get my head around
But long before it was achieved by John Lennon and his
three mates
McGonagall, the terrible weaver poet from Dundee crossed
the Atlantic with dreams of making it big in The States

I try to picture him walking, in his own odd way
Chapping on every theatre door on and off Broadway

Every day he walked up and down times square with
pamphlets to hawk
But like a soup that would not boil, he failed to reduce his stock
For, while the punters were intrigued by his rather peculiar
manner
They would simply not buy a book with his much beloved
royal banner

CHORUS: *Howdy Mr McMonogal, I say your books would carry much more*
appeal
If you were to remove that god damn royal seal

NARRATOR: Then McGonagall shouted, in terms most certain
That amounted to *"I do beg your bloody pardon"!*

He turned on his heels and stomped off with a thump
After telling the gentleman to take a running jump

He was proud of the royal seal
And the land from which it came
He knew that if they could not accept that
Then he would just have to go hame

The trip continued to be a disaster
But just before he was to vanish
His dear friend he was staying with
Pulled in great favours to arrange a concert for to help his name
establish
But in a perfectly McGonagall move
He refused to perform as it was on the sabbath

37

I can't help but feel that he could have avoided this journey
most strifey
If someone from Dunfermline had told him:

CHORUS: We've a Carnegie Hall in Fife, eh

NARRATOR: It must have been hard to give up on another dream to
return to his Dundee tenement
Not least of all because it surely meant
Having to perform for his vicious fans
Where he would take his life into his hands

Vicious Fans

Each time he returned the stage
The mob really upped the ante
Taking sheer abuse
Was becoming his modus operandi
Once night he was drenched in herring guts and scampi
To say the least he would have been reekin
Then, another night in Breechin
He was dressed all fancy like Clarke Gable
Well they cut his coat tails off for a souvenir and nailed his hat
to a table

He was chased off stage almost every night
He'd fear for his future
He'd bang on door in the street begging for someone to let him hide
in their grocery shop or butchers

But this was his fate, accepted it
This was life in Dundee
He needed the mob more than they needed he

And I'm sure that any doctor that bore witness to it
That they would not advise even the healthiest of men to go
through it.

And so his health declines, so bad he can't even sell his
pamphlets in the street
And he's left writing grovelling letters to wealthy men to help
him make ends meet

He complains of pains, of noises in the head
The doctor explains he should rest up in bed.

B: "I'll tell you what is ailing ye
You're writing too much poetry
I must advise from your refrains that you refrain
Because you're suffering from too much swelling of the brain"

NARRATOR: He didn't stop writing works both poetic and dramatical
But from appearing on stage he took a three year sabbatical

He doesn't leave the house
He certainly couldn't perform
So can you imagine the mob's excitement
When he was to make his return?

Every night they'd rush the stage
While he tried to read his verses
The only venues that could house these animals
Were the big top circuses

He would stand there and take every kind of heckle.
He'd endure endless abuse; verbal, physical and mental
If it meant that he'd walk away with but a single shekel

To deter the audience from actions most sinister
He requested for, along with his pay
The presence of a minister
This was something that was not provided
And so with all sorts of missiles he collided
These ruffians, roustabouts and boisterous vandals
Threw their pies, their fish, their pish and their sandals
He was pelted with soot, flour bombs and red wine
Then he was forced to utter the eternal line

"Gentlemen, I beg
No more rotten eggs"

Or was it

"Gentlemen please
No more garden peas"

Either way, it was comedy gold
Until they started throwing bricks and he was knocked out cold

Exile

This was the last time he would perform in Dundee
Not his choice, he was happy, well, at least with the fee

You see he could handle the abuse,
In that respect he seemed a pro
And I suppose we'll just never know
If he got tougher skin in that regard
Watching his parents find life so hard

You see that settle, flee, settle, flee, settle, flee notion I
mentioned early on could sound romantic
But the chances are it would have been terribly frantic

For they didn't just move because they were discontent
But were chased out of town because of their Irish accent

Perhaps, having seen them push on, he's inherited their resolve
And so a problem like abuse he could surely solve
With just a little protection from city forces
So what happened next was perplexing, even remorseless

You see it wasn't just audiences who wanted to give him a doin'
Dundee City Council had their own plan stewing

For, rather than see an ageing poet is given protection and rest
They'd rather be seen to be dealing with civic unrest

CHORUS: *Any theatre that had the Bard on their boards*
Would not get their license restored

NARRATOR: So, a ridiculed, abused poet, sixty-four years of age
Rather than get protected, is effectively banned from the
Dundee stage

And though he pleaded his case
The ban stayed enforced
And when he threatened to sue
The case was simply ignored

Some friends rallied round
Tried to get him a state pension
For, as Mick Hucknell would say:
Money's too tight to mention

But the worst part of the ban
Worse than the loss of wage
Was that now he couldn't go up on stage
There was no controlled space for the mobs to let out their rage

So now he was baited in the streets
He begged magistrates
To have police protection on their beats.

CHORUS: *"There goes mad McGonagall*
Let's spit at him and chase him and pelt him with stones
Let's call him all sorts of names and chase him back home
And if he stays in the house and that seems boring
Let's all go down to Paton's Lane and kick his tenement door in"

NARRATOR: And perhaps once again he thought of his father and his
mother when speaking the line
"When you're persecuted in one town you flee to another"

"Welcome! Welcome thrice! to the year 1893
The year I intend to leave Dundee
Why, for the way it has treated me"

CHORUS: But he must have wanted to stay a little more
Because he didn't actually leave until 1894

Life after Dundee

NARRATOR: The first place he settled after he decided to give
Dundee a permanent wide berth
Was Perth

The people seemed nicer
He could happily walk down the street
But gigs were few and far between
And he couldn't sell enough pamphlets to eat

So he spent the last six years of life in sorrow
Where he was born, in Edinburgh

The move started strong
With big shows that were very appreciative and much less outrageous
He was beginning to think his last few years could be quite lucrative
Like when Elton John retired to Vegas

But while they were a civil bunch
And for that he had to salute them
He discovered that, while they may they have had more cash
It was much harder to get it out them

And he couldn't shake the hoaxers
In Edinburgh they tried to make him look one hell-oh-a-cunt
When they staged a lavish ceremony at the university,
unveiling him as 'Sir' William 'Topaz' McGonngall; Knight of
the White Burmese Elephant

And so his health declined in Edinburgh
Along with his finances
He seldom leaves his flat
But for the briefest of glances

He keeps abreast of goings on in Dundee
Though his ban is never lifted
So from his impoverished life in Edinburgh
He is never shifted

The Weekly News though, who started it all
At the end did show some willing
They set up a benevolent fund in his name
And it only raised six shillings

He could tell it was the end
He'd travelled each and every highway
But more much more than this
He did it his way.

Epilogue

How does a self taught poet
Who achieved global superfame
Get buried like his parents
In a pauper's grave with no name?

And if you think that seems cruel that this is the end he got
Well, he would have died poor anyway, that's a weaver's lot
He tried for something different, he gave it a shot
And though he didn't get fortune with his fame
At least he died a poor mug at his own game

So what do we say about a man like this
Whose life's work is generally enjoyed because it's pish
Even your humble narrator must confess
That I'm no better than the rest

That my joy,
Like how we are transfixed by the asteroid
Or how we contemplate the void
Comes from a place of schadenfreude

Laughing with or laughing at
I just can't seem to answer that

Does that kind hatred goes in
Through a deep rooted kind of social osmosis
Surely it would deplete the spirit
Unless he was short of a diagnosis
And I say that with full understanding

That respect for mental health conditions
In the Victorian era was in need of reprimanding

Did he just have to?
Like, did he just have to do it?
Was there some deeper force that drove him to it?

Or, over our eyes was he pulling the woollies
Or did he swallow his creative desires and play to please
the bullies

If he carved out success in spite of the meanness
Then frankly I think he's a genius

How do you begin to eulogise
When all artists can be so varyingly scrutinised

And not just artists but art as well
Take this show for example
Some of you will have found it swell
But for others it might have been a living hell

It might have tugged on your heart
While perhaps you wish you'd taken your chance to leave at
the start

So the question can't be as simple as if he was bad or good
Or how much of his appeal he misunderstood

No it can't be as simple as good or bad
But should we not look at the impact he had

Did he honestly think as he sat there by the Tay
That his name would survive to this day?

Okay, he may have never been the poet Laureate of the
era of the Victorians
But he's been spoken about since by many historians
And the fact that we still speak about him shows
That he's eclipsed many of his poetical heroes
And while he might not be best pleased to know how,
compared to his contemporaries, he's critically measured
I hope he's delighted that he's still remembered

I like to think of him there as he lies
With a life lived flashing before his eyes

Wether he was trying his best and was simply rubbish
Or if he felt he was truly gifted and needed to flourish
Whether he was good, bad, funny, at it, I don't think it really
matters
For pushing through your struggle for the dream that's in your
heart is
For me, the real test of a true artist

So go, tell his story, tell it far and wide
Make your friends laugh, have them burst at the side
Just please don't forget the real man inside

PLAY ENDS

SELECTED POEMS

By William McGonagall

THE RAILWAY BRIDGE OF THE SILVERY TAY

Beautiful Railway Bridge of the Silvery Tay!
With your numerous arches and pillars in so grand array
And your central girders, which seem to the eye
To be almost towering to the sky.
The greatest wonder of the day,
And a great beautification to the River Tay,
Most beautiful to be seen,
Near by Dundee and the Magdalen Green.

Beautiful Railway Bridge of the Silvery Tay!
That has caused the Emperor of Brazil to leave
His home far away, incognito in his dress,
And view thee ere he passed along en route to Inverness.

Beautiful Railway Bridge of the Silvery Tay!
The longest of the present day
That has ever crossed o'er a tidal river stream,
Most gigantic to be seen,
Near by Dundee and the Magdalen Green.

Beautiful Railway Bridge of the Silvery Tay !
Which will cause great rejoicing on the opening day
And hundreds of people will come from far away,
Also the Queen, most gorgeous to be seen,
Near by Dundee and the Magdalen Green.

Beautiful Railway Bridge of the Silvery Tay!
And prosperity to Provost Cox, who has given
Thirty thousand pounds and upwards away
In helping to erect the Bridge of the Tay,

Most handsome to be seen,
Near by Dundee and the Magdalen Green.

Beautiful Railway Bridge of the Silvery Tay!
I hope that God will protect all passengers
By night and by day,
And that no accident will befall them while crossing
The Bridge of the Silvery Tay,
For that would be most awful to be seen
Near by Dundee and the Magdalen Green.

Beautiful Railway Bridge of the Silvery Tay!
And prosperity to Messrs Bouche and Grothe,
The famous engineers of the present day,
Who have succeeded in erecting
The Railway Bridge of the Silvery Tay,
Which stands unequalled to be seen
Near by Dundee and the Magdalen Green.

THE FAMOUS TAY WHALE

'TWAS in the month of December, and in the year 1883,
That a monster whale came to Dundee,
Resolved for a few days to sport and play,
And devour the small fishes in the silvery Tay.

So the monster whale did sport and play
Among the innocent little fishes in the beautiful Tay,
Until he was seen by some men one day,
And they resolved to catch him without delay.

When it came to be known a whale was seen in the Tay,
Some men began to talk and to say,
We must try and catch this monster of a whale,
So come on, brave boys, and never say fail.

Then the people together in crowds did run,
Resolved to capture the whale and to have some fun!
So small boats were launched on the silvery Tay,
While the monster of the deep did sport and play.

Oh! it was a most fearful and beautiful sight,
To see it lashing the water with its tail all its might,
And making the water ascend like a shower of hail,
With one lash of its ugly and mighty tail.

Then the water did descend on the men in the boats,
Which wet their trousers and also their coats;
But it only made them the more determined to catch the whale,
But the whale shook at them his tail.

Then the whale began to puff and to blow,
While the men and the boats after him did go,
Armed well with harpoons for the fray,
Which they fired at him without dismay.

And they laughed and grinned just like wild baboons,
While they fired at him their sharp harpoons:
But when struck with, the harpoons he dived below,
Which filled his pursuers' hearts with woe.

Because they guessed they had lost a prize,
Which caused the tears to well up in their eyes;
And in that their anticipations were only right,
Because he sped on to Stonehaven with all his might:

And was first seen by the crew of a Gourdon fishing boat
Which they thought was a big coble upturned afloat;
But when they drew near they saw it was a whale,
So they resolved to tow it ashore without fail.

So they got a rope from each boat tied round his tail,
And landed their burden at Stonehaven without fail;
And when the people saw it their voices they did raise,
Declaring that the brave fishermen deserved great praise.

And my opinion is that God sent the whale in time of need,
No matter what other people may think or what is their creed;
I know fishermen in general are often very poor,
And God in His goodness sent it drive poverty from their door.

So Mr John Wood has bought it for two hundred and
twenty-six pound,
And has brought it to Dundee all safe and all sound;

Which measures 40 feet in length from the snout to the tail,
So I advise the people far and near to see it without fail.

Then hurrah! for the mighty monster whale,
Which has got 17 feet 4 inches from tip to tip of a tail!
Which can be seen for a sixpence or a shilling,
That is to say, if the people all are willing.

THE MOON

Beautiful Moon, with thy silvery light,
Thou seemest most charming to my sight;
As I gaze upon thee in the sky so high,
A tear of joy does moisten mine eye.

Beautiful Moon, with thy silvery light,
Thou cheerest the Esquimau in the night;
For thou lettest him see to harpoon the fish,
And with them he makes a dainty dish.

Beautiful Moon, with thy silvery light,
Thou cheerest the fox in the night,
And lettest him see to steal the grey goose away
Out of the farm-yard from a stack of hay.

Beautiful Moon, with thy silvery light,
Thou cheerest the farmer in the night,
and makes his heart beat high with delight
As he views his crops by the light in the night.

Beautiful Moon, with thy silvery light,
Thou cheerest the eagle in the night,
And lettest him see to devour his prey
And carry it to his nest away.

Beautiful Moon, with thy silvery light,
Thou cheerest the mariner in the night
As he paces the deck alone,
Thinking of his dear friends at home.

Beautiful Moon, with thy silvery light,
Thou cheerest the weary traveller in the night;
For thou lightest up the wayside around
To him when he is homeward bound.

Beautiful Moon, with thy silvery light,
Thou cheerest the lovers in the night
As they walk through the shady groves alone,
Making love to each other before they go home.

Beautiful Moon, with thy silvery light,
Thou cheerest the poacher in the night;
For thou lettest him see to set his snares
To catch the rabbit and the hares.

THE SORROWS OF THE BLIND

PITY the sorrows of the poor blind,
For they can but little comfort find;
As they walk along the street,
They know not where to put their feet.
They are deprived of that earthly joy
Of seeing either man, woman, or boy;
Sad and lonely through the world they go,
Not knowing a friend from a foe:
Nor the difference betwixt day and night,
For the want of their eyesight;
The blind mother cannot see her darling boy,
That was once her soul's joy.
By day and night,
Since she lost her precious sight;
To her the world seems dark and drear,
And she can find no comfort here.
She once found pleasure in reading books,
But now pale and careworn are her looks.
Since she has lost her eyesight,
Everything seems wrong and nothing right.

The face of nature, with all its beauties and livery green,
Appears to the blind just like a dream.
All things beautiful have vanished from their sight,
Which were once their heart's delight.
The blind father cannot see his beautiful child, nor wife,
That was once the joy of his life;
That he was wont to see at morn and night,
When he had his eyesight.
All comfort has vanished from him now,
And a dejected look hangs on his brow.

Kind Christians all, both great and small,
Pity the sorrows of the blind,
They can but little comfort find;
Therefore we ought to be content with our lot,
And for the eyesight we have got,
And pray to God both day and night
To preserve our eyesight;
To be always willing to help the blind in their distress,
And the Lord will surely bless
And guard us by night and day,
And remember us at the judgment day.

LINES IN DEFENCE OF THE STAGE

Good people of high and low degree,
I pray ye all be advised by me,
And don't believe what the clergy doth say,
That by going to the theatre you will be led astray.

No, in the theatre we see vice punished and virtue
rewarded,
The villain either hanged or shot, and his career retarded;
Therefore the theatre is useful in every way,
And has no inducement to lead the people astray.

Because therein we see the end of the bad men,
Which must appall the audience – deny it who can
Which will help to retard them from going astray,
While witnessing in a theatre a moral play.

The theatre ought to be encouraged in every respect,
Because example is better than precept,
And is bound to have a greater effect
On the minds of theatre-goers in every respect.

Sometimes in theatres, guilty creatures there have been
Struck to the soul by the cunning of the scene;
By witnessing a play wherein murder is enacted,
They were proven to be murderers, they felt so distracted,

And left the theatre, they felt so much fear,
Such has been the case, so says Shakespeare.
And such is my opinion, I will venture to say,
That murderers will quake with fear on seeing murder in a play.

Hamlet discovered his father's murderer by a play
That he composed for the purpose, without dismay,
And the king, his uncle, couldn't endure to see that play,
And he withdrew from the scene without delay.

And by that play the murder was found out,
And clearly proven, without any doubt;
Therefore, stage representation has a greater effect
On the minds of the people than religious precept.

We see in Shakespeare's tragedy of Othello, which is sublime,
Cassio losing his lieutenancy through drinking wine;
And, in delirium and grief, he exclaims –
"Oh, that men should put an enemy in their mouths to steal
away their brains!"

A young man in London went to the theatre one night
To see the play of George Barnwell, and he got a great fright;
He saw George Barnwell murder his uncle in the play,
And he had resolved to murder his uncle, but was stricken
with dismay.

But when he saw George Barnwell was to be hung
The dread of murdering his uncle tenaciously to him clung,
That he couldn't murder and rob his uncle dear,
Because the play he saw enacted filled his heart with fear.

And, in conclusion, I will say without dismay,
Visit the theatre without delay,
Because the theatre is a school of morality,
And hasn't the least tendency to lead to prodigality.

THE DEMON DRINK

Oh, thou demon Drink, thou fell destroyer;
Thou curse of society, and its greatest annoyer.
What hast thou done to society, let me think?
I answer thou hast caused the most of ills, thou demon Drink.

Thou causeth the mother to neglect her child,
Also the father to act as he were wild,
So that he neglects his loving wife and family dear,
By spending his earnings foolishly on whisky, rum and beer.

And after spending his earnings foolishly he beats his
wife-
The man that promised to protect her during life-
And so the man would if there was no drink in society,
For seldom a man beats his wife in a state of sobriety.

And if he does, perhaps he finds his wife fou',
Then that causes, no doubt, a great hullaballo;
When he finds his wife drunk he begins to frown,
And in a fury of passion he knocks her down.

And in that knock down she fractures her head,
And perhaps the poor wife she is killed dead,
Whereas, if there was no strong drink to be got,
To be killed wouldn't have been the poor wife's lot.

Then the unfortunate husband is arrested and cast into
jail,
And sadly his fate he does bewail;
And he curses the hour that ever was born,
And paces his cell up and down very forlorn.

And when the day of his trial draws near,
No doubt for the murdering of his wife he drops a tear,
And he exclaims, "Oh, thou demon Drink, through thee I
must die,"
And on the scaffold he warns the people from drink to fly,

Because whenever a father or a mother takes to drink,
Step by step on in crime they do sink,
Until their children loses all affection for them,
And in justice we cannot their children condemn.

The man that gets drunk is little else than a fool,
And is in the habit, no doubt, of advocating for Home Rule;
But the best Home Rule for him, as far as I can understand,
Is the abolition of strong drink from the land.

And the men that get drunk in general wants Home Rule;
But such men, I rather think, should keep their heads cool,
And try and learn more sense, I most earnestly do pray,
And help to get strong drink abolished without delay.

If drink was abolished how many peaceful homes would
there be,
Just, for instance in the beautiful town of Dundee;
then this world would be heaven, whereas it's a hell,
An the people would have more peace in it to dwell

Alas! strong drink makes men and women fanatics,
And helps to fill our prisons and lunatics;
And if there was no strong drink such cases wouldn't be,
Which would be a very glad sight for all Christians to see.

O admit, a man may be a very good man,
But in my opinion he cannot be a true Christian
As long as he partakes of strong drink,
The more that he may differently think.

But no matter what he thinks, I say nay,
For by taking it he helps to lead his brother astray,
Whereas, if he didn't drink, he would help to reform society,
And we would soon do away with all inebriety.

Then, for the sake of society and the Church of God,
Let each one try to abolish it at home and abroad;
Then poverty and crime would decrease and be at a stand,
And Christ's Kingdom would soon be established throughout
the land.

Therefore, brothers and sisters, pause and think,
And try to abolish the foul fiend, Drink.
Let such doctrine be taught in church and school,
That the abolition of strong drink is the only Home Rule.

Fellow men! why should the lords try to despise
And prohibit women from having the benefit of the
parliamentary Franchise?
When they pay the same taxes as you and me,
I consider they ought to have the same liberty.

And I consider if they are not allowed the same liberty,
From taxation every one of them should be set free;
And if they are not, it is really very unfair,
And an act of injustice I most solemnly declare.

Women, farmers, have no protection as the law now stands;
And many of them have lost their property and lands,
And have been turned out of their beautiful farms
By the unjust laws of the land and the sheriffs' alarms.

And in my opinion, such treatment is very cruel;
And fair play, 'tis said, is a precious jewel;
But such treatment causes women to fret and to dote,
Because they are deprived of the parliamentary Franchise vote.

In my opinion, what a man pays for he certainly should get;
And if he does not, he will certainly fret;
And why wouldn't women do the very same?
Therefore, to demand the parliamentary Franchise they are
not to blame.

Therefore let them gather, and demand the
parliamentary Franchise;
And I'm sure no reasonable man will their actions despise,

For trying to obtain the privileges most unjustly withheld from
them;
Which Mr. Gladstone will certainly encourage and never
condemn.

And as for the working women, many are driven to the
point of starvation,
All through the tendency of the legislation;
Besides, upon members of parliament they have no claim
As a deputation, which is a very great shame.

Yes, the Home Secretary of the present day,
Against working women's deputations, has always said- nay;
Because they haven't got the parliamentary Franchise-,
That is the reason why he does them despise.

And that, in my opinion, is really very unjust;
But the time is not far distant, I most earnestly trust,
When women will have a parliamentary vote,
And many of them, I hope, will wear a better petticoat.

And I hope that God will aid them in this enterprise,
And enable them to obtain the parliamentary Franchise;
And rally together, and make a bold stand,
And demand the parliamentary Franchise throughout Scotland.

And do not rest day nor night-
Because your demands are only right
In the eyes of reasonable men, and God's eyesight;
And Heaven, I'm sure, will defend the right.

Therefore go on brave women! and never fear,
Although your case may seem dark and drear,
And put your trust in God, for He is strong;
And ye will gain the parliamentary Franchise before very long.

THE TAY BRIDGE DISASTER

Beautiful Railway Bridge of the Silv'ry Tay!
Alas! I am very sorry to say
That ninety lives have been taken away
On the last Sabbath day of 1879,
Which will be remember'd for a very long time.

'Twas about seven o'clock at night,
And the wind it blew with all its might,
And the rain came pouring down,
And the dark clouds seem'd to frown,
And the Demon of the air seem'd to say –
"I'll blow down the Bridge of Tay."

When the train left Edinburgh
The passengers' hearts were light and felt no sorrow,
But Boreas blew a terrific gale,
Which made their hearts for to quail,
And many of the passengers with fear did say –
"I hope God will send us safe across the Bridge of Tay."

But when the train came near to Wormit Bay,
Boreas he did loud and angry bray,
And shook the central girders of the Bridge of Tay
On the last Sabbath day of 1879,
Which will be remember'd for a very long time.

So the train sped on with all its might,
And Bonnie Dundee soon hove in sight,
And the passengers' hearts felt light,
Thinking they would enjoy themselves on the New Year,

With their friends at home they lov'd most dear,
And wish them all a happy New Year.

So the train mov'd slowly along the Bridge of Tay,
Until it was about midway,
Then the central girders with a crash gave way,
And down went the train and passengers into the Tay!
The Storm Fiend did loudly bray,
Because ninety lives had been taken away,
On the last Sabbath day of 1879,
Which will be remember'd for a very long time.

As soon as the catastrophe came to be known
The alarm from mouth to mouth was blown,
And the cry rang out all o'er the town,
Good Heavens! the Tay Bridge is blown down,
And a passenger train from Edinburgh,
Which fill'd all the peoples hearts with sorrow,
And made them for to turn pale,
Because none of the passengers were sav'd to tell the tale
How the disaster happen'd on the last Sabbath day of 1879,
Which will be remember'd for a very long time.

It must have been an awful sight,
To witness in the dusky moonlight,
While the Storm Fiend did laugh, and angry did bray,
Along the Railway Bridge of the Silv'ry Tay,
Oh! ill-fated Bridge of the Silv'ry Tay,
I must now conclude my lay
By telling the world fearlessly without the least dismay,
That your central girders would not have given way,
At least many sensible men do say,
Had they been supported on each side with buttresses,

At least many sensible men confesses,
For the stronger we our houses do build,
The less chance we have of being killed.

MODERN MCGONAGALLS

By Gary McNair via the spirit of William McGonagall

ROYAL WEDDING

Rejoice! There is to be a royal wedding
For a great celebration the country is heading
Which Royal, you ask, is due to marry?
It's her majesty's grandson, Harry.

Many people will be pleased to see Harry wed
And they will hope it will help put his silly behaviour to bed
He has often attracted bad press from the paparazzi
Like the time he dressed up as a … German soldier.
And though he will likely never wear the crown
We're all rather pleased to see him settle down

And his bride, most beautiful to be seen
Will be the newest relative of the Queen
You may recognise her due to one main factor
She's been on the telly where she works as an actor
She's not the woman that plays Miss Marple
She's in that show Suits, and her name's Meghan Markle

To see a royal on their wedding day
Should make all our hearts merry and gay
I dare say not even the republicans would smirk
As we will all be given the day off work

AN ODE TO PROFESSOR STEPHEN HAWKING

It was on the 14th of March in the 18th year of this millennium
That the world bade farewell to one of its greatest craniums
He was often seen down the planetarium
But sadly we'll not be seeing any mair o' him

Raise a toast
Charge your glasses at a lock-in
Fly the flag at have mast
For Professor Stephen Hawking

He understood the universe more than most
But he was a humble man who did not like to boast
He didn't need big fancy titles to prove he was right good
Perhaps that is why he refused a knighthood

He sold nearly as many books as Mantel and Gaiman
Explaining the complexities of physics and time to the layman
Famed for his mind and his electronic voice
His cameo roles in popular shows like The Simpsons did
make people rejoice

It would have made people's hearts heavy with dismay
When he left this world in the month of March and on the 14th day
It was a sad day indeed as he wasn't the only one going
He left us on the same day as Bullseye's Jim Bowen

THE BEAST FROM THE EAST

The good people of Scotland were visited this winter by a
terribly snowy beast
A storm which has been named The Beast From The East
With a snow level that seemed to increase and increase
Like a loaf in the in the oven that has too much yeast

It snowed so much that when the beast did blow
Houses and cars were covered in snow
And what's even more surprising –
The snow level just kept on rising

Oh how boreas did blow and did bray
Freezing many Scottish rivers from the Clyde to the Tay
Many cars and trains did prove to be inferior
When trying to drive through the snow from Siberia

But on the beast continued to blow and bray
And with its howl did seem to say
That in the house you should stay
For at least a couple of days

People did struggle to make a homemade feast
As many of the nation's supply lines had ceased
It was hard to get eggs, milk or even bread for a piece
The people did search their freezers hoping they'd stowed
away a pie or a quiche

And if someone looked as though they were soon to
become deceased
You would struggle to get a hold of a priest

Oh how people wished they could be released
From howling wind and snow of The Beast From The East

No Planes Took Off
No Trains Were Running
But the white covered streets
Were simply stunning

TRUMP CANCELS VISIT

The current president of the United States has cancelled
his trip to UK
Because he doesn't like where we moved their embassy
He says this is the real reason for cancelling his visit
But many of us are asking … is it?

Perhaps he thought it wise to avoid the bad press
Or the chance of his visit sparking civic unrest and protest
For we live in an age where feedback is immediate
And the people of this great nation will be quick to tell him
he's an eejit

It would be easy for me to make fun of the man
For his bewildering haircut or his satsuma tan
His terrible golf swing, his enormous waist
His gauche interiors showing terrible taste
His limited language and poor sense of humour
Or the fact that his face looks like a malignant tumour

Yes we could focus on these surface facts
But I'd rather take issue with the way he acts

He boils the blood of any good human
With the way that he openly disregards women
He calls respectable media outlets fake news
When they don't agree with his narrow views
He annoyed all and sundry
When he tried to stop Muslims entering the country

Some say Theresa May should not have offered the place
And now that he has cancelled she has egg on her face

She could have pleased her people by rescinding his invite
But she was too scared to do what was right
Some say this was her chance to look strong and stable
But in this simple task she is clearly not able
And though his decision to stay away may not last ad infinitum
This poet is certainly glad he's not coming to the United Kingdom.

THE OPENING OF THE V & A IN DUNDEE

It was in the year 2018 and on the 17th day of September
That the people of Dundee were given a day to remember
It will be remembered as a fine and glorious day
The day they opened Dundee's V&A

The cutting edge museum and art gallery is just great
Designed by Kengo Kuma and Associates
Everyone in the town does agree it is lovely
And it sits really well beside the RSS Discovery

The building will display works of beautiful art
That will inspire the mind and also the heart
And what's more admission is completely free
This gem will surely attract visitors from near and far to Dundee

For Dundee is a city with a growing reputation
And the council must expect the V&A to bring people flooding
from near and far to the city through the railway station
But the whole plan to bring tourists to the city may be
doomed to fail
Because of the extortionate inter city train fares set by Scot Rail

From Glasgow you may think:
"Great, it's only 1hr and 20minutes away, that's quite short, eh?"
But unbelievably that journey will cost you £38.40!

How can they justify this assault on people's purses
It will force people onto the roads in cars and in buses
Or worse, on their journey, they may not even depart
And so they may not ever sample Dundee's glorious art

This poet fears that without the temptation for people to
travel from both near and afar
Dundee's V&A will be destined to be no more than a
glorified cafe and bar
For what's the point of trying to show the world all your culture
If tourists are being kept away by fat cat vultures